W9-AXR-472

Through the Eyes of CHILDREN

TURKEY

Connie Bickman

Published by Abdo & Daughters, 4940 Viking Drive, Suite 622, Edina, Minnesota 55435.

Library bound edition distributed by Rockbottom Books, Pentagon Tower, P.O. Box 36036, Minneapolis, Minnesota 55435.

Printed in the United States.

Cover Photo credit: Connie Bickman, GeoIMAGERY
Interior Photo credits: Connie Bickman, GeoIMAGERY
Bettmann, pages 5 and 6
Map created by John Hamilton

Edited by Julie Berg

LIBRARY OF CONGRESS CATALOGING-IN-PUBLICATION DATA

Bickman, Connie.
    Turkey / Connie Bickman.
        p.   cm. -- (Through the Eyes of Children)
    Includes index and glossary.
    ISBN 1-56239-327-8
    1. Children--Turkey--Social life and customs--juvenile literature.
    2. Turkey--Social life and customs--Juvenile literature.
    [1. Turkey--Social life and customs.]   I. Title. II. Series.
    DR432 B   1994
    956.1--dc20   94-14801
                                        CIP
                                        AC

Contents

Introduction

If you visit Turkey you will come away smiling.
The people there are very friendly.
They smile at you and ask you if you would like to have some tea.
Everywhere you go, people give you glasses of tea.
Tea with square pieces of sugar to make it sweet.
You are to put the sugar lump in your mouth.
You leave it in your mouth until the tea melts it away.
It is a different way to drink tea.
But they are happy when you try it their way.

Customs are different in Turkey.
If you do not know about their food you can go in the kitchen.
They will show you kettles with cooking food.
You can point to what you want.
They will bring it to you.
When you are done eating they sprinkle rose water on your hands.
It is to cleanse your hands and to say thank you for the food.

Turkey has many modern cities.
They are filled with art of the past and of today.
Paintings, tiles, weavings and other art tell the history of Turkey.
Many of the buildings look like sculptures themselves.

Turkey is an important country.
It is sometimes referred to as a bridge.
This is because it lies between Europe and Asia.

The city of Istanbul has a river running through it.
It is called the Bosphorus Strait.
Part of Istanbul is in Europe and part of it is in Asia.

Turkey is surrounded by water on three sides—
the Mediterranean, the Aegean Sea, and the Black Sea.
So it is a busy country and
has many beautiful coastlines and beaches.

Turkey also has many tall mountains and beautiful valleys.
It has rivers and lakes and rich farmland.

Turkey's borders touch many other countries:
Syria, Russia, Iran, Iraq, Bulgaria, and Greece.
It has many neighbors!

TURKEY

Istanbul

Bursa

Ankara

Izmir

Eskisehir

Kizil River

Konya

Kayseri

Mersin (Icel)   Adana

Gaziantep   Diyarbakir

100 miles

Population
55.4 Million

Area (square miles)
301,381

City Population
- Over 1 million
- Over 500,000
- Over 100,000
- Under 100,000

Capital: Ankara

Meet the Children of Turkey

This girl is wearing a carsaf.
It is like wrapping yourself in a blanket.
Only your eyes would be showing.
She is dressed like this because of her religion.
She is Muslim.
Under her drape she wears clothes just like you do.

These girls live
in a big city.
They have fun
playing with
each other.
They like to play jumprope.
They like some of the same toys you do.
Most of them have many brothers and sisters.
Sometimes more than one family lives in a house.

This girl is washing dishes.
Many families live together in this house.
The house has three rooms.
The food is cooked in the small kitchen.
One room is for eating and visiting.
The third room is for sleeping.

These girls are
friends.
They have
made jewelry
and orna-
ments.
They want to
sell them.
Many children
sell things
they have
made.
They need to
find ways to
make money
for their families.

These girls live in a small village.
All around the village are big
volcanoes.
It is windy there.
The wind blows volcano dust all
over.
It is hard to stay clean in this
village.
These children don't have many
toys.
They don't have TV's or radios.
They make up their own games.
They have fun playing with their
friends.

What's Good to Eat?

A food named kebab is very good to eat in Turkey.
It is vegetables and meat cooked on a stick.
There are many kinds of kebab.
Have you ever eaten shish-kebab?
Everyone drinks tea in Turkey.
There are many places to drink tea. They are called tea gardens.

This is a flat bread.
You tear off a piece of bread and dip it in goat cheese.
You can also dip it in the yogurt.
It tastes different than your bread.
Do you think you would like it?

Do you buy your food in the super-market?
Most of the food in Turkey is sold in open markets.
These markets are on the streets.
This boy is selling water-melon from his fruit cart.

What do you think this boy is selling?
It is food.
It is lamb meat wrapped in a thin layer of crust.
It tastes good.

Where Do They Live?

Children in the cities live in houses and apartments.
Some children live in mud and brick houses.

This is a Nomad village.
These people are called nomads because they move often.
They move when the seasons change.
They move when they need more food for their animals.
They cook and eat all together in one tent.
The other tents are their homes.

This girl lives in the Nomad village.
Do you see the pretty bright beads?
She made the necklace herself.

What Do They Wear?

Children wear bright, colorful clothes.
Do you have favorite colors you like to wear?
These girls just washed some wool in the river.
They are hitting the wool with sticks.
This helps to get the water out.
They will stretch the wool out in the sun to dry.
Then they will dye it different colors.
Some of it will be made into yarn.
The yarn will be used to knit clothing.
It will also be used to make carpets.

This woman looks like she is wearing a potato sack over her head—but it's not.
In each area of Turkey, women drape in different materials.
It is their religious tradition.

This grandmother is wearing a scarf over her head and face.
It is part of her religion also.
She is holding her granddaughter.
Do you like the pretty clothes she knit for the baby?
The women in this village like to knit.
They make sweaters and hats and stockings.
The children learn to knit when they are very small.

How Do They Work?

Children begin to work when they are very small.
They must help their families.
This young boy is helping his father in the field.
They are making a rope.
The rope is made from the hay they are cutting.
The father adds hay to the end of the rope.
The boy turns a crank that twists the hay.
This makes a strong rope.
They use the rope to tie the rolls of hay.
This boy lives in the eastern part of Turkey.
He is a Kurdish farm boy.

These children are getting water.
They don't have a sink and faucet like you do.
They go to the well to wash.
They fill buckets with water to bring home for cooking.

Farming is hard work in Turkey.
Few people have tractors.
These boys do their farm work with oxen.
The wagon is handmade from wood—
even the wheels!

This boy is working in the city.
He is selling rolls.
He can balance the tray of bread on his head!

Animals are Friends

Goats and lambs are favorite pets.
Would you like a pet goat?
Lambs and goats are more than pets in Turkey.
When this lamb gets bigger its wool will be
sheared to make yarn.
Its wool will grow back.
It will still be a good pet for this boy.

23

School is Fun!

Children in the country are often taught by their parents.
City children go to schools like you do.
They learn to read, write, and to make carpets.
Girls, ages 10 to 16, work on a carpet every day.
It takes two or three years to finish a carpet.
Then the carpet is sold.
The money goes to help support the school.
When the girl graduates she is given a loom.
Then she can make her own carpets.
She also is given an assignment.
She has to teach one other person how to make a carpet.
This way handmade carpets will continue to be an art in Turkey.

This girl is in school.
She studies part of the day just like you do.
Part of her schoolwork is learning to make
carpets.

What are Traditions?

Making carpets is also a family traditon.
Every member of the family works on the carpet.
This boy is finishing a rug.
He is tying ends and trimming the yarn.
The carpet will be sold in his uncle's carpet shop
in Istanbul.

Making carpets is a tradition in Turkey.
They have been made there for many,
many years.
Can you think of any traditions you have?

Getting Around

Cars, buses, and trucks are driven in Turkey.
Wooden carts pulled by horses are also popular.
Streets are made of dirt and also concrete.
Many children and adults ride bikes in Turkey.
It is faster than walking.
It is also cheaper than buying a car.

Horses are often used for traveling.
They are also used for farming.
These horses are going home after a long day in the field.

Just For Fun!

Children like to jump rope and play with
squirt guns.
They like to run and play.
They like to be happy.
They are just like you!
Does this boy look like your neighbor?
This boy is dressed in jeans, a T-shirt and
sunglasses—
but is wearing a red turbin on his head.

Their Land

The land in Turkey is very different from one end to the other.
It has mountains with beautiful tall trees and valleys.
It also has flat, dry dusty plains.
It has beautiful beaches from three seas.
They are the Black Sea, the Mediterranean Sea and the Aegean Sea.

Do you see the big mountain?
It is called Mount Ararat (AIR-uh-rat).
In Turkey it is called Agri Dagi (AH-gree DAH-gee).
This is where people believe Noah's Ark is buried.
It takes four days to climb this big mountain.

Life in the City

Ankara is the capital of Turkey.
Istanbul is another very old city.
It is modern in many ways.
But in many parts it still looks like it did a
long time ago.

This is a bakery wagon.
Big sticks of bread are put in wood crates.
They are brought to the stores on open wagons.
The bread is made fresh every day.

This is a famous building.
It is a castle in southeastern
Turkey.
It is beautiful inside and outside.
People visit the castle everyday.
Nobody lives in the castle now.
It is very old.

These boys are having fun.
They are riding their horse
through an old city.
The city is called Old Van.
It once had a huge castle
on top of the hill.
Now the city is almost
gone.
There are only a few build-
ings and walls left.
There is a new city called
Van, right next to the old
city.

Family Living

Many children have families just like you do.
They go to movies and have picnics and play games.
Other children live in houses with many other families.
They all help to take care of each other.

The women of this house are washing the clothes.

This little boy is helping his mother.
He is helping to dye wool.
It is a messy job.
He doesn't care.
He is having fun.

Children are the same everywhere

It is fun to see how children in other countries live. Many children have similar ways of doing things. Did you see things that were the same as in your life? They may play and go to school and have families just like you. They may work, travel and dress different than you.

One thing is always the same. That is a smile. If you smile at other children, they will smile back. That is how you make new friends. It's fun to have new friends all over the world!

Glossary

Carsaf - full-length robe with a hood and veils.

Loom - an apparatus for weaving cloth.

Muslim - a believer in the religion of Islam.

Turbin - a scarf wrapped around head.

Tradition - beliefs carried on from family to family.

Istanbul - a city in Turkey.

Index

About the Author/Photographer

Connie Bickman is a photojournalist whose photography has won regional and international awards.

She is retired from a ten-year newspaper career and currently owns her own portrait studio and art gallery. She is an active freelance photographer and writer whose passion it is to travel the far corners of the world in search of adventure and the opportunity to photograph native cultures.

She is a member of the National Press Association and the Minnesota Newspaper Photographers Association.